transfer

images on glass, fabric, ceramic, stone,
paper, metal, plastic, and wood

Isabel de Cordova
Photography by Sue Wilson

LAUREL
GLEN

contents

RIGHT *Star anise is a beautiful spice that looks great transferred onto shot glasses.*

introduction

Transferred images are the latest way to decorate your home. Whether you want to put some patterns on your bed linen, or capture the colors of autumn leaves on a lampshade, transfers let you personalize your home in a unique and stylish way. You can use photographs, line drawings, music, letters, and even real flowers and leaves as your subjects; just look around for inspiration.

The aim of this book is to show how to transform everyday objects, from tableware to cushions, and even computer mouse pads, into stunning individual originals. By using transfers, you can customize a variety of surfaces, including fabric, ceramics, metal, wood, plastic, stone, and glass. You can do as little or much as you like—whether you want to create an eye-catching centerpiece for a table, an accent piece for the living room, or even a matching set of curtains, cushions, and bed linen to create a total theme for a room.

As you do your normal shopping and flick through lifestyle magazines, you will see that photographic images have been applied to a wide variety of products and that the use of transfers in decoration has become a very popular style in recent years. This is an easy way to create a new look in your home.

The great advantage of using transfers is that the techniques involved are very easy, and you do not need to be an artist because there is no drawing involved. The process is simple and provides an easy way to personalize household items—whether for your own use or as unique gifts to give to friends and family. Some projects are more time-consuming than others—it will take longer to make the Curtains of falling petals (see page 22) than the Fishbowl vase (see page 54), for example—and some are a little detailed, but all are quite simple to make.

One of the best things about transferring is that it allows you to use personal photographs and images. I love the idea of being able to display pictures in an interesting way. You could put pictures of your family on coffee mugs or a child's drawing on a bedside lamp. But even if you'd rather keep your vacation pictures in a drawer, transferring can still be for you. There are plenty of inanimate images that would make ideal transfers. You could, for example, photocopy a flower or a leaf and use that as your transferred image. The end of the book features some of the images I used to make the projects featured in this book. Just remember, though, that you don't have to use them, you can use any image you like. Transferring is a very personal technique, so you should think carefully and choose images that suit your individual style.

There are sixteen projects in this book, each with clear step-by-step instructions covering all the different ways to transfer an image. Once you have a feel for them, I hope you will feel inspired to experiment on your own.

ISABEL DE CORDOVA

getting started

materials and surfaces

You can transfer images onto all sorts of materials, allowing you to decorate your home and make inventive personalized gifts. Throughout the book you will find examples of all the various transferring techniques, plus details of the surfaces for which they are suitable. Here is a quick reference guide to the various methods.

There are a number of ways to transfer an image onto a surface, but the basic theory remains the same. Color-photocopy your chosen image on the shiny side of some transfer paper. There are then various methods of attaching the transfer paper to surfaces such as ceramic, glass, fabric, wood, metal, paper, and plastic.

The linen shoe bag is the only project not to use transfer paper, using instead transfer paste to move ink from a color-photocopy onto fabric.

You will find suppliers for the wet-release transfer paper and the transfer paste on page 96.

Transferring methods

Simple wet release transfer paper

This method can be used on paper, plastic, glass, ceramics, fabric covered canvases, and metal. Simply immerse the transfer paper images in water or dab them with a wet sponge, then slide off the backing paper and attach the picture to your chosen surface. Glass, metal, and ceramic can then be baked in a warm oven to further secure the transfers, but they will not be dishwasherproof.

Wet release transfer paper with turpentine

This method can be used on paper, plastic, wood, and stone. It is done by applying a thin layer of turpentine to the surface where the transfer will go and then applying the wet-release transfer paper. If the surface is quite rough, partially fill a pump action spray with turpentine and lightly mist the transfer. This helps the image melt into the nooks and crannies.

Wet-release transfer paper with glue

Used on absorbent surfaces such as canvas and paper, this method is the same as the wet-release transfer paper method except for the fact that a thin layer of 50 percent water-diluted white craft glue is brushed on the surface before the transfers are applied. The glue helps the transfers to stick to absorbent surfaces and also makes it easier to adjust the position of the transfers.

Iron-on wet-release transfer paper

This method also uses wet-release transfer paper, but involves ironing the image onto fabric. The backing paper is then soaked off to reveal the transfer. Since the image is applied to the fabric face down, you will need to flip the image before you begin if you do not want it to appear back-to-front.

Ink-jet printer iron-on transfer paper

This method allows a transfer to be ironed straight onto fabric. The backing paper is then gently peeled off. Ink-jet transfer paper works with almost all ink-jet printers, and it lets you print computer scans straight onto transfer paper. If you do not have a computer, scanner, and ink-jet printer, use the iron-on wet-release transfer paper method instead.

Transfer paste

This method is for use on natural fiber fabric only. Put a piece of foil under the fabric before starting. Lay a trimmed color-photocopied image on another piece of foil. Then, with the image face up, spread transfer paste over the picture. Place the image face down on the fabric and press it down to make sure it has stuck. Remove excess paste, then let it dry.

Use a sponge to soak the backing paper with water; then use your fingertip to gently rub away the backing paper, leaving the image clearly revealed. Leave the transfer to dry; then apply another coat of paste to seal the image.

Surface texture

Generally speaking, it is easiest to transfer images to smooth textured materials. With fabric the best results are achieved when transfers are applied to even weaves, and consequently fabrics with a raised texture, such as terrycloth or velvet, are not suitable for transfers. Fortunately, using wet-release transfer paper with turpentine (see page 10) allows other materials with a slight surface texture, such as wood and stone, to be used as the turpentine makes the transfers melt into the contours of the surface.

Surface color

Since they are slightly transparent, transfers usually work best on a light-colored background. A dark background will inevitably show through the transfer. This effect can sometimes be used deliberately to incorporate the background into the picture, as shown on the Rose pillow (see page 38) and the Wooden tray (see page 62). Remember, however, that a colored transfer on a colored background will result in a third color. If you are not sure what will result from your color mixes, it is wise to test the transfer on a like-colored background before you embark on the real project.

Fabric transfer aftercare

In most cases, a fabric item can be given a gentle hand-wash or be laundered on a delicate cycle. However, always check the transfer manufacturer's directions first. Turn the item inside out before washing it or place it in a fabric bag to protect the image. After washing an article, iron it carefully to set the images, remembering to lay a piece of baking parchment over the image to protect it and prevent it from melting. Do not fold the transfers for storage; this may cause them to crack.

where to find your images

Choosing an image to transfer can be a tricky business. Sometimes an image will present itself as an ideal candidate, but you may have to hunt around. Photographs can be a great source of images, but try to think beyond them to include line drawings, wallpaper, fabric patterns, music, handwriting, and even two-dimensional objects like leaves and feathers.

Choosing an image

Images on any material that can be photocopied or scanned and printed from a computer can be transferred. There are endless possibilities, and you can start by looking around your home for some inspiration. Look through books and magazines, and old photographs, too. Other good source materials can be letters, music scores, memorabilia, children's drawings, paintings, buttons, and natural textures. Look outside and search for leaves and flowers, feathers, shells, and pebbles. You might want to create a theme, based perhaps on a favorite hobby or pastime, such as sports or music.

Copyright

Always make sure the images you use for transferring are not copyrighted. Using postcards or greeting cards from art galleries and elsewhere, for example, is not advisable. It is easy to tell whether the copyright of an image is owned by an individual or a company because it will feature the symbol © plus the owner's name either in the corner, on the back, or—in the case of an extended publication—in a list of credits and acknowledgments. Fortunately, there are publications available that provide copyright-free images that can be copied for personal use (see page 96).

image styles and manipulation

Once you have chosen an image, there are a number of ways you can manipulate it, should you so desire. You can, of course, use the original image, but if you're feeling a little more creative, there are plenty of other options.

Reducing and enlarging

Altering the size of an image is an easy way to create variation if you intend to use it more than once on a project. A small and large version of an image side by side can make a charming composition. By using a photocopier or computer scanner, you can reduce or enlarge your pictures to suit your design. Remember, though, if you increase the size of your image by more than 100 percent, you will begin to notice a reduction in picture quality, particularly if it includes a high level of fine detail. Similarly, if you drastically reduce the size of a picture, the details will begin to merge.

Repeat images

Deliberately repeating an image is an easy way to bring a cohesive element to your design. The effect will vary according to the way you place the repeated images. Multiple images can look quite intense on a small object, such as on the plate opposite with leaves fanning out around its edge, but when teamed with the less structured design of the plate below from the same set, its intensity is toned down and works as a unifying design element.

If a repeated image is placed at regular intervals, it becomes a pattern. If you're going to do this, think carefully about where you want to place the transferred images and calculate how many copies you will need. Make a few extra, just in case.

Overlapping images

You can use the slightly translucent nature of transfer paper to your advantage when laying down your images. By overlapping the transfers, you can create a multilayered image. This technique works best used sparingly or the pictures can become quite confused. Nevertheless, it is ideal for illustrating delicate images, such as the skeletal leaves shown on these plates.

If your chosen transferred images are colored, overlapping them will result in further variations of color. Get it right and you can produce jewel-like effects. If you are unsure how well colors will work when they are overlapped, experiment on a similarly colored surface before you begin.

Tints

If you have access to a computer scanner, you will be able to alter the color of your chosen images. You can also do this on a color photocopier, although the range of possible color variations will be more limited. If the project on which you're working needs to fit in with the color scheme of a room, for example, this means that you can adapt your image to suit. So, whether you prefer subtle complementary color variations or bold, eye-catching shades, you can adapt your images to suit your taste.

Flipping images

Another way to add variety to your transfers is to flip the original pictures. If you want to do this, you will need access to a computer, scanner, and color printer, as a photocopier does not allow you to flip images. The resulting mirror image can be used to add variety to your designs. Placing mirror images side by side is a dramatic way to make a feature of flipped pictures. It draws the eye to their meeting point and gives an impression of regularity and order.

Some of the projects in this book, such as those that use iron-on methods or transfer paste, flip images as part of the transferring process. This does not usually matter unless the picture contains elements that need to appear the correct way around. Think carefully about the images you use in these instances since images containing text, people, and buildings, for example, might need to be flipped before they are photocopied.

Adjoining images

If your design incorporates more than one transfer, you may need to master the technique of laying them down edge to edge. Both the simple wet-release transfer paper method and the wet-release transfer paper with turpentine method allow you to adjust the position of transfers when you first apply them. The best way to achieve a neat fit in this case is to place the transfer close to its final position and then to slide it gently into place. Iron-on methods require a little more precision; you will need to make sure the edges of transfers are precisely aligned before you apply the iron.

When ironing a design in place, it can be tricky to make sure all the edges have stuck to the fabric. When ironing transfers edge to edge, take care not to iron over an uncovered image—it will melt and stick to the base of your iron. A double layer of baking parchment can be used as a temporary barrier between the iron and existing transfers.

Spot color

If you do not have access to a computer and scanner, there are still ways to alter specific elements of pictures dramatically. The plate opposite shows a picture in the bottom right-hand corner that has been altered to make it seem as though the little girl is wearing a bright orange dress. This dramatic effect is actually quite simple to achieve.

First trace the outline of the dress on tracing paper, then photocopy the black-and-white picture and a square of your chosen color on transfer paper. Place the traced dress over the square of colored transfer paper and use it as a template to cut out a colored dress shape. Make sure you use a piece of masking tape to stop the image from slipping once you have begun cutting.

When you have attached the black-and-white transfer to the plate, transfer the colored dress shape on top. The result is a limited area of color on an otherwise black-and-white image.

Sepia

If you use sepia film in your camera, you will find that your photographs have an atmosphere that color pictures lack. Perhaps it is because they hark back to a bygone era, but sepia images look fantastic transferred onto household items since they seem to capture a mood as much as an image.

I particularly like to place sepia images next to ordinary black-and-white images, as shown opposite. If you have access to a computer, scanner, and printer, you can manipulate ordinary photographs to give them a sepia tint.

projects

Fill your window with petals

cascading down from the ceiling to the floor. These delicate gauze curtains work as a discreet screen, bringing both privacy and style. As the sun shines through them, the curtains cast a hint of the petals' warm color over your room.

Try to fit as many copies of the petals as possible on the transfer paper—you will be surprised how many you will need. To add an extra creative dimension, you could enlarge and reduce the original petal a fraction to give you different sizes with which to work.

I chose this cascading effect because of the way it draws the eye down the curtain. To do this, place a few petals near the top of the curtains and then arrange the rest in a random pattern as though they are falling from the ceiling. At the very bottom of the curtains, position a few petals on their sides—as if they have reached the ground and settled there.

Hang your curtains in a window that receives the morning sun, open the window slightly to allow the breeze to waft through the fabric, and their full fairytale quality will be brought to life.

curtains of falling petals

You will need

Materials

Pressed petals or pictures of petals
(see page 87)

Access to a color photocopier

Lazertran transfer paper

Utility knife and cutting mat, or a pair
of scissors

Pair of sheer 100 percent cotton
curtains

Masking tape

Ironing board

Iron

Small shallow bowl

Sponge

Baking parchment

Technique

Iron-on wet-release transfer paper
(see page 10)

1 First decide whether you want to photocopy real petals, or the pictures of petals on page 87. Try to fit as many petals on to one sheet of paper as possible—you could use a computer and scanner to aid this process, or you could color-photocopy the petals a number of times, then cut them out and stick them on a blank sheet of paper. Bear in mind that the images will appear reversed on the finished curtains. Color-copy the sheet of petals onto the shiny side of a piece of transfer paper, then carefully cut them out using either a utility knife on a cutting mat, or scissors. To decide on the position of the petals, lay the first curtain flat on a table and anchor the images with pieces of masking tape (see page 48). When you are happy with the position of the petals, place the curtain on an ironing board. One at a time, turn the petals face down (flipping the images) and, using a warm iron and a circular motion, press them into position. Continue until all the pieces are secure.

2 Lay the curtain on a clean waterproof surface. Fill a small shallow bowl with water, then sponge water onto the petal transfer's backing paper. When the water has been absorbed and the paper looks less opaque, it will begin to lift off or curl back. Gently peel off the backing paper from the transfer and sponge off any excess white glue. Repeat this process with the rest of the petals.

3 When the fabric is dry, lay the curtains on the ironing board with the images face up. Place a piece of baking parchment on top of the first few petals. Then, using a warm iron and a circular motion, as before, iron the fabric for a couple of minutes to seal the transfers. Take care not to accidentally iron over an uncovered image—it will melt and stick to the base of the iron. Continue until the images sink into the fabric. (The curtains should be ironed this way, using the baking parchment, every time they are washed, to secure the transfers.) Repeat the process with the second curtain.

Transform a favorite picture

into a unique work of art by transferring it to stretched canvas. Whether you choose a family picture or even a vacation scene, this stylish project lets you add a personal touch to the photographs you display around your home.

Since the canvas becomes such a feature of the project, there is no need for a picture frame, and the final result would certainly merit a place

canvas art

on your mantelpiece. If you use a sepia picture, it should fit well in a traditional or modern setting, a grand house or a modest apartment.

Transferring to canvas is an extremely easy process, and once you have mastered it, you could well be inspired to make a whole set of prints for your living room. A nice idea is to make extra copies to give to your friends and family as gifts to remember a special occasion.

You will need

Materials

Acrylic-primed linen canvas—stretched
   over a wooden frame

Sepia photograph

Access to a color photocopier

Lazertran transfer paper

Utility knife, metal ruler, and cutting
   mat, or a pair of scissors

Large shallow tray

Newspaper

50 percent water-diluted white
   craft glue

Large paintbrush

Paper towels

Rolling pin

Soft dry cloth

Clear spray varnish (optional)

Techniques

Wet-release transfer paper with glue
   (see page 10)

1 When choosing your canvas, pick one that has been stretched over a wooden frame or board, giving it a smooth surface texture. Choose a photograph and enlarge it to approximately ½ inch bigger than the canvas so that it overlaps all four edges. Color-photocopy the picture onto the shiny side of a sheet of transfer paper, printing a spare copy in case of mistakes. Trim any excess paper from your transfer, using either a utility knife and metal ruler on a cutting mat, or scissors.

2 Once you have trimmed the transfer to the correct size, simply lower the image face down, wide edge first, into a large shallow tray of lukewarm water. The paper will start to roll up slightly, but you should leave it to soak for a few minutes until it becomes less opaque.

While the transfer paper is soaking in the water, place the linen canvas frame on a layer of newspaper and, using a paintbrush, apply a thin coat of 50 percent water-diluted white glue over the whole canvas.

3 Carefully lift the transfer paper out of the water and lay it face down on a layer of paper towels to remove any surface water. Then, using your index fingers and thumbs, slide the backing paper off slightly, leaving one of the long edges exposed, and lay the image face up (glue side down) slightly overlapping the corresponding edge of the canvas. Carefully center the image, and when you are happy with the position, gently place a rolling pin on top and slowly slide the backing paper out from under the transfer.

Once the image is in place, look closely and expel any air bubbles with a soft dry cloth or the tip of your finger, to make sure the image is completely flat. Carefully prick any stubborn bubbles with a pin and ease the air out. Fold the overhanging transfer over the sides of the canvas frame.

Leave to dry flat for a few hours; then, if you want a matte finish, apply a coat of clear spray varnish, which will also protect the image.

Decorate your bed linen with

patterned strips placed edge-to-edge around its border. If you are feeling creative, you could design your own patterns. Alternatively, for a good source of suitable designs, try the various copyright-free pattern books that are available (see page 96). These patterns can be copied and the colors altered to suit the color scheme of your bedroom.

patterned bed linen

When selecting strips of pattern, remember that longer strips mean you will need to join fewer pieces together, which will save time. You should also consider whether the fact that the pattern will appear flipped on the bed linen is of any concern (if it contains text, for example). If so, flip the image now so it will transfer correctly and "read" right once applied.

This project uses ink-jet printer paper, which allows you to print an image on it directly from an ink-jet printer. If you do not have a computer, scanner, and ink-jet printer, use the iron-on wet-release transfer paper method (see page 10).

You will need

Materials

2 strips of repeatable patterns in
   contrasting colors

Access to a computer, scanner, and ink-
   jet printer

Ink-jet transfer paper

Utility knife and cutting mat, or a pair
   of scissors

Plain pale cotton or cotton-blend
   bed linen

Iron

Marble slab

Baking parchment

Techniques

Ink-jet printer iron-on transfer paper
   (see page 10)

1 Ink-jet printer paper can be used on any cotton or cotton-blend fabric, but a light-colored, smooth-textured fabric gives the best results. Calculate how much pattern you will need to cover your bed linens, scan the pattern with a computer scanner, and try to fit as many strips as possible on each sheet of paper. You can print straight onto the Ink-jet printer transfer paper using the Ink-jet printer. Follow the printer's instructions before printing. Then, using either a utility knife on a cutting mat or a pair of scissors, cut around the edges of the pattern strips, leaving a ¼-inch margin along the long edges.

2 Next prepare to iron the pattern on the edge of the bed linen. Use a marble slab instead of an ironing board—a marble cheese board would be ideal. Place a double layer of ironed scrap material on the marble, then lay the bed linen on top, making sure that both are smooth. Use the hottest iron setting suitable for the fabric, but do not use the steam setting. Lay the transfer face down in place and begin ironing, moving slowly from one end to the other, using firm pressure, and securing all corners.

Once the transfer is secure and the backing paper is cool enough to touch, lift the paper off by peeling it from one end to the other. If a section of pattern has not sealed properly, replace the backing paper and iron over it for a few seconds more.

3 To continue the pattern, repeat step 2 taking care to align the joining edges. When nearing the join, take extra care not to iron over the edge of the paper onto an uncovered image: it would melt and stick to the iron. For extra protection, fold a piece of baking parchment in two and lay it over the seam. Peel off the backing paper, working toward the join.

Apply a second row of pattern the same way, taking care to keep the two lines parallel.

When all the images are in place, reduce the temperature of the iron slightly, put a piece of baking parchment on top of the lines of pattern, and iron all over. This method produces durable, washable results. Remember to turn the bed linen inside out before laundering.

Protect your favorite shoes

in this stylish linen shoe bag. Take a photograph of your best-loved pair of shoes and transfer it to the bag to create a chic visual label. In this instance I made the transferred image as close to the actual size of the shoes as possible, just to add extra impact.

As the iron-on process flips the images, you may want to reverse the picture before you begin transferring—this is essential if there is any writing on the inside of the shoes.

You could continue the theme of this idea to create laundry bags or even storage bags for treasured items. The finished bags look really pretty hanging casually from a doorknob or a hook on the back of your bedroom door.

You can buy solid-colored linen or cotton bags of a suitable size for this project, or—if you have time—you could make your own bags. Do remember to use a material made from natural fibers though since they work best with transfers.

linen shoe bag

You will need

Materials

Photograph of a pair of shoes

Access to a color photocopier

Utility knife and cutting mat, or
    a pair of scissors

Aluminum foil

Linen shoe bag, ironed

Dylon transfer paste

Paintbrush

Iron

Ironing board

Paper towels

Rolling pin

Sponge

Bowl

Techniques

Transfer paste (see page 13)

1 Using transfer paste can be messy, so wear old clothes or an apron while working. When choosing your picture, remember that this method will flip the transferred image, so avoid including any text unless you have a computer and scanner to reverse the image at this early stage.

Color-copy the photograph onto a sheet of plain paper. Cut out the shoes using either a utility knife on a cutting mat or a pair of scissors. Lay the two shoe images face up on a piece of aluminum foil. Squeeze a generous amount of paste onto each image and, using a paintbrush, spread the paste to completely cover the photocopies.

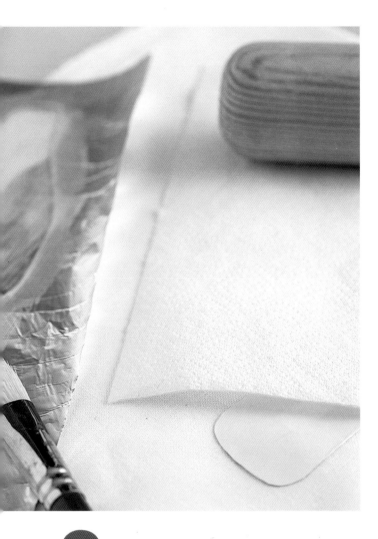

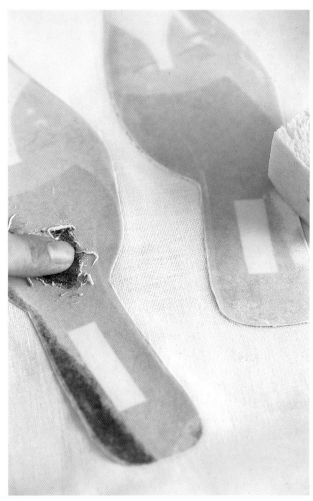

Once the images are completely dry, fill a small bowl with lukewarm water and, using a sponge, soak the paper. Leave for a few minutes. Then, using your fingertip, carefully rub away the paper until the shoes are clearly revealed. Take extra care when rubbing the edges of the image, because they are especially delicate. Leave the shoe bag to dry. Finally, using the paintbrush, apply a thin coat of transfer paste to seal the image. Leave the bag to dry again.

When washing the shoe bag, turn it inside out and launder it on a delicate wash cycle. Always iron the bag on the wrong side—you must never iron directly on the image.

Place a layer of foil inside the linen bag to act as a barrier between the two layers of fabric. Next, when the transfer paste has sunk into the paper, obscuring the images, carefully pick up the first transfer and lay it face down on the fabric. Press the image down firmly, making sure that there are no wrinkles in the fabric. Then place a paper towel on top and, using a rolling pin, lightly press the transfer, rolling in all directions for about a minute to make sure all the edges have adhered. If any excess paste seeps out, uncover the image and remove the excess paste with paper towels. Repeat with the second shoe. Leave to dry for a minimum of four hours, but preferably overnight.

Transfers can be overlapped

to give a dramatic multilayered effect. It sounds complicated, but is actually very simple. Just pick a colored background image and a black-and-white photograph. If you overlap the two images, the white areas of the photograph will take on the colors of the background image. This is a useful method if you want to add color to a black-and-white image or if you want to pick out

rose pillow

just a little of the color scheme of your room. It lets you create subtle color highlights without becoming overpowering.

For your transfer background, use a simple block of color, a patterned fabric, or go for something textural such as velvet, wood, or beaten copper. Make the background image slightly larger than the rose picture in order to create a casual frame effect.

A set of pillows decorated with roses would make an eye-catching display on a plain sofa or arranged on a bed.

You will need

Materials

Square black-and-white image of
a rose (see page 92), or image of
your choice

Square background image(s) of your
choice, such as velvet, wood, or
gold leaf

Access to a color photocopier

Lazertran transfer paper

Utility knife, metal ruler, and cutting
mat, or a pair of scissors

Plain cotton pillow cover

Ironing board

Iron

Plastic chopping board

Sponge

Baking parchment

Technique

Iron-on wet-release transfer paper
(see page 10)

1 Start by choosing two images you would like to overlay—in this case, a black-and-white rose and a closeup picture of some wood were used. You will need at least four color copies of each image—a computer and scanner would aid this process. Alternatively, you could photocopy the images four times and stick them on a sheet of paper.

Photocopy the sheet of images on the shiny side of transfer paper. Cut out the images using either a utility knife and metal ruler on a cutting mat, or a pair of scissors, making sure the background images are slightly larger than the rose picture. Then place your pillow cover onthe ironing board and position a background transfer face down (flipping the image) on the cover. Using a warm iron and a circular motion, iron for a minute or two to secure the image.

3
Place your pillow cover on the ironing board with the background image face up. Position the rose image face down on top of the background. Place the baking parchment over the layered transfers and iron over them to secure the rose picture—the baking parchment will keep the edges of the first transfer from touching the iron. When the rose is in position, repeat step 2.

Repeat the entire process with the remaining images, then cover the transfers with some baking parchment and iron again.

2
Place the plastic chopping board inside the pillow cover. Sponge water onto the backing paper of the background transfer. Leave until the water has been absorbed; the paper will look less opaque and will begin to lift off or curl back. Peel off the backing paper and carefully sponge off any excess white glue, then leave to dry.

Once dry, place the cover on the ironing board with the background image face up. Lay a piece of baking parchment over it and, using a warm iron and a circular motion, press until the image sinks into the cloth. Leave it to cool.

Design your own plates by

transferring images of mouth-watering food onto them. You will find that a smooth, flat china surface is the best for transfers as it is much easier to work on; if your china has a raised edge, you may find that you have some difficulty laying the transfer across the uneven surface, so try to limit your transfers to the flat areas. Simple white plates give a wonderful crisp look to the finished design, but pale-colored plates can also be embellished with transfers.

When you are deciding on the images you wish to transfer, remember that transfer paper tears quite easily, so try to choose images that have an uncomplicated edge.

I particularly enjoy the humor of putting food images on plates. Here I have decorated some breakfast plates with images of croissants and rolls, but there are endless possibilities. You could make a set of dessert plates showing images of delicious cakes, or decorate side plates with a colorful salad. Would a plate of tempting chocolates be too cruel?

breakfast plates

You will need

Materials

Picture of a croissant (see page 89)

Picture of sliced toast (see page 89)

Picture of a torn roll (see page 89)

Access to a color photocopier

Lazertran transfer paper

6 plain ceramic plates, cleaned to
    remove any traces of grease

Utility knife and cutting mat, or a pair of
    scissors

Large shallow tray

Sponge

Paper towels

Soft dry cloth

Oven

Technique

Simple wet-release transfer paper
    (see page 10)

Make two color photocopies of the three images, plus some spares in case of mistakes. Try to fit them all onto one sheet of paper—you could use a computer and scanner to aid this process, or simply color-copy the images, cut them out, and glue them on a blank sheet of paper. Set the photocopier's toner density on high before color-photocopying onto the shiny side of the transfer paper—this helps give the image a solid appearance when it is applied to the plates.

Cut out the transfers using either a utility knife on a cutting mat, or scissors. Be especially careful cutting out the roll; it has some intricate small details. Transfer paper is transparent, so you can leave some strips between the roll and the crumbs to keep them connected.

2 Lower each image, face down, into a large shallow tray of lukewarm water, or you can soak them individually with a wet sponge. The paper will start to roll up slightly, but leave it in the water until it becomes less opaque. Lift the images out and place them on paper towels to remove excess surface water. Carefully slide off a little of the backing paper between your index fingers and thumbs. Take care when doing this as transfer paper can tear easily. Having eased off a small amount of backing paper, place the transfer in position face up (glue side down) on the plate and slowly pull the backing paper out from under the transfer. When the image is in place, use a soft dry cloth, to carefully expel any air bubbles to make sure the image is flat. Prick any stubborn air bubbles with a pin and ease the air out with your finger.

3 When you have stuck all the transfers on the plates, leave them to dry for at least 24 hours. They can then be put in a warm oven (350° F) for about 10 minutes until the transfers melt and harden into an enamel. The heat process secures the images and makes them completely waterproof and virtually scratchproof.

As shown here, you can use pictures of almost any type of food to make this project. I used pictures of scones and cupcakes to make an alternative set of dessert plates. Alternative images can be found on pages 86–93.

Give pasta a twist by serving

it in a bowl decorated with a quirky design. The pasta shapes provide a wonderful source of transfer images—there are so many different and interesting shapes from which to choose. Look in cookbooks, on pasta packaging, or refer to the back of this book (page 90) for ideas.

Concentrate on the outside of the bowl and arrange the images so the pasta shapes can be seen on all sides. Make sure your design is balanced around the whole bowl, since it will be the centerpiece at the table. Using masking tape to position the individual pieces gives you the opportunity to play with the design before you actually commit yourself. Try placing the shapes in different positions: do you prefer a busy-looking design or a minimalist approach? This is your chance to try them out.

You could continue the theme on individual pasta bowls. I prefer to keep the design of the small bowls simple, so I placed a single image below each bowl's rim and another inside— allowing guests to discover the "extra" pasta just as they finish their meal.

pasta serving bowl

You will need

Materials

Pictures of different pasta shapes (from
    cookbooks or see page 90)

Access to a color photocopier

Lazertran transfer paper

Large plain ceramic serving bowl,
    cleaned to remove any traces
    of grease

Utility knife and cutting mat, or a pair of
    scissors

Masking tape

Shallow bowl

Paper towels

Soft dry cloth

Oven

Technique

Simple wet-release transfer paper
    (see page 10)

1 Make a rough calculation of the number of pasta shapes you will need to decorate your bowl and try to fit them all onto one sheet of paper, adding a few extra in case of mistakes. You could use a computer and scanner to aid this process, or simply color-photocopy the pasta shapes a number of times, then cut them out and glue them on a blank sheet of paper. Color-photocopy the sheet of pasta images onto the shiny side of some transfer paper. Set the toner density on high before photo-copying; this helps give the images a solid appearance when they are applied to ceramic objects. Cut the transfers out carefully using either a utility knife on a cutting mat, or scissors.

2 Decide where to position the pasta images by temporarily attaching them to the bowl with masking tape. Once you are pleased with your design, remove the masking tape from a couple of images and lower them face down into a bowl of lukewarm water to soak. The paper will start to roll up slightly, but leave it until it becomes less opaque.

Lift an image out of the water and dab it on a paper towel to remove any surface water; then carefully slide off a little of the backing paper between your index finger and thumb. Place the transfer in position face up (glue side down) on the bowl and slowly pull the backing paper out from under it. Carefully expel any air bubbles with a soft dry cloth. Repeat with the remaining transfers.

3 When all the pasta shapes are in place around the bowl, leave them to dry for 24 hours. The bowl can then be put in a warm oven (350° F) for 10 minutes until the transfers melt and harden into an enamel. This process secures the images and makes them completely waterproof and virtually scratchproof.

As shown, you don't have to limit yourself just to decorating a serving bowl; you can make a complete set by placing an image in the bottom of some smaller bowls as well.

Using a closeup picture of a

cactus plant on a glass vase gives the vase's smooth surface the impression of texture. The graphic quality of the transferred cactus looks fantastic on its own, but you could go one step further and fill the vase with fine sand to give the image more depth of color.

Use the vase as part of a display, as shown here, by including some thin white candles to

cactus vase

contrast with the beautiful colors of the cactus. Another way to show the pretty purple color of the vase would be to fill it with glass beads. It would also look great filled with a stylish selection of contemporary sculptural flowers.

If you love plants, but are not blessed with a green thumb, this vase is a great way to bring a little extra organic color into your home without actually having to care for a real plant.

You will need

Materials

Closeup picture of a cactus or
    other plant

Access to a color photocopier

Large rectangular clear glass vase,
    cleaned to remove any traces
    of grease

Lazertran transfer paper

Paper towels

Utility knife, metal ruler, and cutting mat,
    or a pair of scissors

Large shallow tray

Newspaper

Soft cloth

Oven

Technique

Simple wet-release transfer paper
    (see page 10)

1 Enlarge your chosen image until it is big enough to cover at least one side of the vase. If the vase is small enough to let you wrap an image around more than one side, print it large enough to do so and thus avoid unnecessary transfer "seams" later. Set the toner density on high before color-photocopying onto the shiny side of some transfer paper—this helps give the image a more solid appearance when it is applied to glass. Print enough copies to cover the vase, plus an extra in case of mistakes. Trim your transfers to fit neatly on the sides of the vase, using either a utility knife and metal ruler on a cutting mat, or scissors. Lower the first image face down, wide edge first, into a large shallow tray of lukewarm water. The paper will start to roll up slightly, but leave it for a few minutes until it becomes less opaque.

3 When the vase is complete, leave it to dry for 24 hours. Then put it in a warm oven (350° F) for about 10 minutes until the transfers melt and harden into an enamel. This will secure the images and make them completely waterproof and virtually scratchproof.

You can use closeup photos of any kind of plant. Good alternative images to use are bamboo and grass reeds, as shown below. Their textural qualities make striking vases.

2 Once the transfer paper has been immersed long enough, carefully lift it out of the water and lay it face down on a layer of paper towels to remove excess surface water.

Place the vase on its side on some newspaper. Using your index fingers and thumbs, slide the backing paper off slightly from the top edge and lay the transfer face up (glue side down) along the top edge of the vase. Adjust the position of the image very carefully as transfer paper can tear easily, and make sure the top edge of the image lines up exactly with the rim of the vase. Then hold the backing paper with one hand and hold down the transfer with the other, and slowly slide the backing paper out from under the transfer. Use a soft cloth to expel any air bubbles that appear as you lay the transfer down. Carefully prick any stubborn bubbles with a pin and then gently ease the air out using the tip of your finger.

When you have completed the front of the vase, turn it over and repeat the process on the next side. If you have decided to wrap the transfer around more than one side of the vase, take extra care as you mold the transfer around the corners.

Things are not as they seem

on this witty glass vase. Transfers of goldfish have been used to add a little humor to the design. The fish images are quite intricate, so you may find that cutting them out will be a tricky job, but the end result is definitely worth the effort.

Continue the theme inside the vase, if you wish, by transferring some pebble images on to the base. As an alternative, you could add a few water plants on the sides of the vase. Let your imagination run wild until you are completely happy with the design, but try not to let the images become cluttered, or you may find that they detract from the flowers you intend to display in the vase.

Here I have half-filled the vase with water and added a few bright orange amaryllis blooms. I like the quirkiness of this arrangement, since the idea of fish swimming around the flower stems appeals to my sense of humor. It looks just as good if you fill the vase with water and simply float a few flower heads on the surface.

fishbowl vase

You will need

Materials

Pictures of 2 goldfish (see page 88)

Access to a color photocopier

Lazertran transfer paper

Utility knife and cutting mat, or a pair
of scissors

Clear glass globe vase

Masking tape

Shallow bowl

Sponge

Paper towels

Oven

Technique

Simple wet-release transfer paper
(see page 10)

1 Color-photocopy the two goldfish images onto the shiny side of a sheet of transfer paper. You may want to include some extra copies, in case of mistakes. Set the photocopier's toner density on high—this will help give the images a more solid appearance when they are transferred to glass. To use transfer paper on non-absorbent shiny surfaces like glass, no glue is needed other than the gum on the back of the paper, but before you start transferring, clean the surface to remove any traces of grease. Carefully trim your transfers to size using either a utility knife on a cutting mat, or a pair of scissors.

3 When the vase is complete, let it dry for 24 hours. It can then be put in a warm oven (350° F) for about 10 minutes until the transfers melt and harden into an enamel. This secures the images and makes them completely waterproof and virtually scratchproof.

You could add more fish or other images such as pebbles. The pebble image shown below was placed inside the vase, which can be tricky to access. This sort of intricate work is best done in two or four sections. Cut around the pebbles and join them one at a time—it will not matter if they overlap slightly.

2 Mark where you want to position the goldfish images by temporarily sticking them onto the surface of the vase with pieces of masking tape. When you are happy with their positions, place the transfers face down in a shallow bowl of lukewarm water; alternatively, you can soak them individually with a wet sponge. Leave the masking tape in place on the vase to mark where you want the transfers to go. The paper will start to roll up slightly, but leave the transfers to soak for a few minutes until the paper becomes less opaque.

Carefully lift the first transfer out of the bowl and lay it face down on a layer of paper towels to remove excess surface water. Place the vase in front of you, carefully pick up the transfer and, using your index finger and thumb, slide a little of the backing paper off. Lay the image face up (glue side down) in position on the vase. Then carefully pull the backing paper out from under the transfer, and, if necessary, adjust the position of the image. Expel any air bubbles using the tip of your finger. Repeat with the second fish.

Add a personal touch with

this beautifully decorated plastic tissue box cover—a less fussy alternative to the traditional frilly lace cover. Choose a design for your box that will coordinate with the décor of your room or complement the other items on your dressing table, creating a unified look.

The pictures you use could be just one image repeated on each side of the box or a number of different images. You could photograph your favorite bottles of perfume and transfer the results onto the sides of the box, as shown here. I chose a simple antique perfume bottle for this project because I like its elegant lines, but you could use pictures of the bottles you keep on your dresser. Alternatively, you could use a photograph of some jewelry, or perhaps some shapely lipsticks and makeup brushes.

You could take this project a step further and decorate other containers, such as a child's toy chest or a useful desk tray for the home office.

tissue box

You will need

Materials

4 square images of perfume bottles
  (see page 92)

Access to a color photocopier

Lazertran transfer paper

Utility knife, metal ruler, and cutting mat,
  or a pair of scissors

Plastic box, cleaned to remove any
  traces of grease

Large shallow bowl

Paper towels

Soft cloth (optional)

Clear spray varnish

Technique

Simple wet-release transfer paper
  (see page 10)

1 Most square facial-tissue boxes measure 4½ inches on all sides, but it is wise to measure your box before you begin. Your plastic box must be slightly larger than the tissue box so the cardboard box can fit inside it.

When you have chosen which images you want to feature on the box cover, enlarge or reduce them until they are slightly bigger than one side of the box. Then color-photocopy the images on the shiny side of transfer paper.

Using either a utility knife and metal ruler on a cutting mat, or a pair of scissors, trim any excess paper from the transfers. Take care; transfer paper is very delicate and can tear easily.

To use transfer paper on non-absorbent shiny surfaces like plastic, no glue is needed other than the gum on the back of the paper. Place one of the trimmed images face down in a large shallow bowl filled with lukewarm water and leave it to soak. The paper will start to roll up slightly, but leave it for a few minutes until it becomes less opaque.

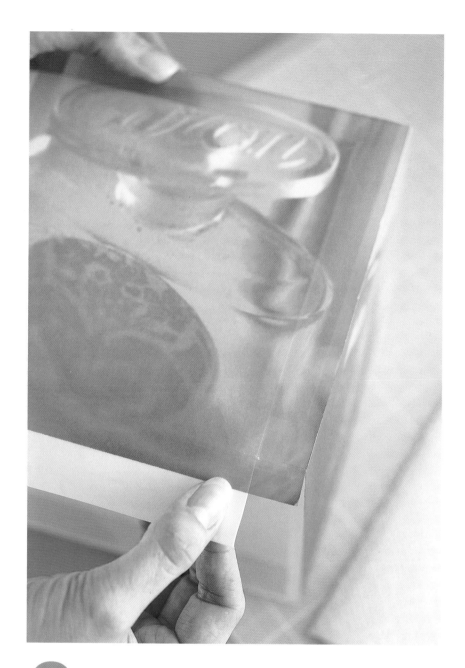

2 Carefully lift the first transfer out of the water and lay it face down on a layer of paper towels to remove the surface water. Place the box on its side in front of you, then with your index fingers and thumbs, carefully slide the backing paper off slightly from one corner and lay the transfer face up (glue side down) centrally on the side of the box.

Hold the backing paper with one hand and hold down the transfer with the other. Gradually slide the backing paper out from under the transfer. Expel any air bubbles with a soft dry cloth or the tip of your finger. Run the blade of a utility knife along the edges of the box to neatly trim off the overhanging edges of the transfer paper.

Repeat the process to cover the remaining three sides of the box; then leave it to dry for 24 hours. Once the transfers are completely dry, spray the box with varnish to protect it from becoming scratched.

3 You can adapt the idea behind this project to other household containers. A simple makeup box, for example, looks great decorated with images of lipsticks and brushes.

Whatever container you make, you will probably find it useful to add a protective layer of spray varnish, particularly if the container is used frequently.

This project works equally well

on a metal or plastic tray, but a light-colored background is usually the most effective since it contrasts with the transferred images. Since transfer paper is so thin, it lends pictures an element of translucency. This characteristic can be used to allow a patterned or textured background, such as the wood of this tray, to show through the lightest areas of the pictures. In this case, the man's white shirt takes on the grain and color of the wood. The warm tones mix well with the original colors of the photograph to give it a sepia-like result.

I chose a series of four pictures for this project, but repeating one image would work as well. The images can be neatly arranged in a rectangle in the center of the tray, as seen here, but it would be equally interesting to place them in a straight line, thus drawing attention to the sequence of movements shown in the photographs.

Alternatively, you could let your imagination go wild and use overlapping images of different sizes to cover the tray.

wooden tray

You will need

Materials

4 action shots (see page 91)

Access to a color photocopier

Lazertran transfer paper

Utility knife, metal ruler, and cutting
   mat, or a pair of scissors

Wooden tray

Ruler

Masking tape

2 shallow bowls

Pure turpentine

Small sponge roller

Paper towels

Soft dry cloth

Pump-action spray bottle (optional)

Clear spray varnish (optional)

Technique

Wet-release transfer paper with
   turpentine (see page 10)

1 First choose a series of four photographs—action shots work particularly well. Here pictures of a chef taking advantage of a few spare moments to eat his lunch have been used.

As this technique calls for turpentine, wear old clothes or an apron, and make sure the room is well ventilated. Copy your chosen pictures on the shiny side of a sheet of transfer paper. Trim all four images to the same size using either a utility knife and metal ruler on a cutting mat, or a pair of scissors. Use a ruler to measure where the pictures should go so they sit right in the center of the tray. The four pictures should fit edge to edge to make a large rectangle.

3 Repeat the transfer process with the remaining three images. Once the pictures are in place and you have removed all of the air bubbles, leave the tray to dry flat overnight. You will then notice that the transfers will begin to melt and sink (migrate) into the surface.

When the transfers are almost dry, you will be able to judge how well they have set. If necessary, spray them with a fine mist of turpentine to finish off the process. A pump-action spray bottle is ideal for this job. Take care not to apply too much turpentine or the images will break up.

If you are likely to use the tray regularly, it is a good idea to apply a thin layer of clear spray varnish to protect the transfers from becoming scratched. Apply the varnish before you remove the masking tape from the surface of the tray.

2 Once you have measured where the four pictures will go, mask around all four sides of the collage area with strips of masking tape, leaving a blank space in the center of the tray where the images will be placed. Then lower the images one at a time into a shallow bowl of lukewarm water. The transfers will start to roll up, but leave them to soak for a few minutes until they become less opaque.

Meanwhile, pour some pure turpentine into a second shallow bowl and, using a sponge roller, lightly roll a thin layer of turpentine onto the masked-off area in the center of the tray. Lift the transfers out of the water and lay them face down on paper towels to remove excess water. Using your index fingers and thumbs, ease a bit of the backing paper off and lay the first image face up (glue side down) in position. Carefully slide the backing paper out while smoothing out any bubbles using a soft dry cloth.

Transfers tear easily and stick to turpentine quite quickly, so take extra care not to break the image if you need to adjust its position.

If you look to nature when designing your projects, you will find that it helps you to find harmonious color combinations. The color palette of fall, when leaves are turning, can be absolutely stunning. The skeletal leaves used in this project have a beautiful cobweb-like delicacy, but you don't have to wait until the fall to collect them since many craft outlets and some gift stores sell them in small packs.

autumnal lampshade

The paper-stretching technique explained in this project is necessary whenever you use wet-release transfers on paper; it stops the paper from wrinkling when the wet transfer is applied. The process is actually very simple, but it does involve a little preparation.

Paper stretching involves a type of gum tape that becomes sticky when dampened. It is used to tape damp paper to a stiff board and dries at the same rate as the paper while the board keeps everything flat. For details of where to buy gum tape, please refer to the suppliers' list on page 96.

You will need

Materials

Utility knife, metal ruler, and cutting mat

Sheet of heavy watercolor paper

Cylindrical wire lampshade frame

Large wooden board

Gum tape

Sponge

Skeletal leaf (or see page 86)

Access to a color photocopier

Lazertran transfer paper

2 small bowls

50 percent water-diluted white craft glue

Paintbrush

Paper towels

Soft dry cloth

Double-sided tape

Fire-resistant spray

Technique

Water-release transfer paper with glue
   (see page 10)

As this technique involves the use of craft glue, wear old clothes or an apron while working. First, using a utility knife and metal ruler, cut the watercolor paper to a size about ¾ inch larger than you will need to wrap around the wire lampshade frame.

Next stretch your paper. To do this, first lay the watercolor paper on a large wooden board, leaving a border of at least 4 inches all around. Next, dampen the glued side of the gum tape and stick it firmly along all the edges of the paper (about ¾ inch from the edge). The gum tape will anchor the paper to the board. Using a sponge, wet the paper and gum tape. The paper will start to ripple, but this is fine.

Leave the paper overnight, by which time it will be completely flat again. Meanwhile, work out your design for the lampshade.

2 Calculate how many leaf images you will need to cover the whole of the lampshade; then try to fit them all on one sheet of paper—you could use a computer and scanner to aid this process, or simply color-photocopy the leaves a number of times. Then carefully cut them out and glue them to a blank sheet of paper.

Change the color of the leaves if you wish. This can be done by scanning the leaf images and manipulating the color with a computer or, to a lesser extent, by altering the color levels on a color photocopier. Color-copy the sheet of leaves on the shiny side of transfer paper.

Cut out the images using a utility knife on a cutting mat. Pour some 50 percent water-diluted white craft glue into a small bowl and brush a thin layer on the paper.

3 Place a couple of leaves in a bowl of lukewarm water and leave them to soak for a few minutes until the paper becomes less opaque and curls up. One at a time, carefully lift the transfers out of the water and lay them face down on a layer of paper towels to remove excess moisture. Using your index finger and thumb, begin to slide the backing paper off and position the tip of the leaf face up (glue side down) on the tacky paper, then slowly slide the backing paper out from under the transfer. Expel any air bubbles with the tip of your finger to make sure the image has adhered completely. Prick any stubborn bubbles with a pin and ease the air out with a soft dry cloth or your fingers. Repeat with the remaining leaves; then let it dry.

When dry, using a utility knife and metal ruler, trim the gum tape from around all four edges of the sheet of paper. Lay it face down on a table and place the wire lampshade frame on top. Then wrap the paper around the frame and join the seam with double-sided tape. For safety, coat the lampshade inside and out with fire-resistant spray.

Forget boring labels on your kitchen storage containers and go for images instead. What else could be contained in this canister but the tastiest selection of cookies? This project provides the perfect way to spruce up your tins and add interest to your kitchen.

Cookie tins are regularly in and out of the cabinet, especially if you have a young family, so baking the tin in a warm oven to render the

cookie tin

transfer waterproof and virtually scratchproof is a great idea. Try to find a tin without a rubber seal under the lid since this is unsuitable for the oven. Otherwise, you could simply decorate the main container and leave the lid unadorned.

You could extend this idea to other storage containers: a jar of coffee beans or a tea caddy, for example. If you intend to use the pictures as labels, try to select easily identifiable images. Alternatively, use text—you wouldn't want to reach for a jar of sugar and end up with salt!

You will need

Materials

Pictures of cookies (see page 89)

Access to a color photocopier

Lazertran transfer paper

Utility knife and cutting mat, or a pair
of scissors

Large shallow bowl

Metal cookie tin, cleaned to remove
any traces of grease

Soft cloth

Paper towels

Oven

Technique

Simple wet-release transfer paper
(see page 10)

1 Color-photocopy both the picture of the stack of cookies and the single cookie making sure they will fit on the side and lid of the cookie tin, respectively. Set the toner density on high and color-photocopy the images on the shiny side of a sheet of transfer paper—this gives the images a more solid appearance when applied to metal. Print a couple of copies in case of mistakes; then trim around the edge of the cookies using either a utility knife on a cutting mat, or a pair of scissors.

2 Once they are trimmed, simply lower the cookie images, face down, into a large shallow bowl filled with lukewarm water and leave them to soak. The paper will start to roll up slightly, but leave the transfers for a few minutes until they become less opaque. Once they have soaked, carefully lift the transfers out of the water and lay them face down on paper towels to remove any surface water.

3 Place the metal tin on its side on a soft cloth to stop it from rolling around while you are positioning the transfer. Gently ease off the backing paper from the large transfer and, remembering that the image can slide, carefully position it face up (glue side down) on the side of the cookie tin. Once the image is in place, carefully expel any air bubbles using a soft cloth. Do the same with the picture of the single cookie, placing it on the lid.

Leave the two cookie transfers to dry; this will take about 24 hours. Then, leaving the tin open, put it in a warm oven (350° F) for approximately 10 minutes until the transfers melt and harden into an enamel. The heat process secures the transferred cookie images, making them completely waterproof and virtually scratchproof. Always wash the tin by hand.

Organic materials have a

simple beauty that complements most interiors. Just light the candle in this cubic stone holder and watch the shadows play across the room.

The Latin phrases on the sides of the candleholder give the illusion of having been carved into the surface of the stone, but this is not the case. By using transfers on stone, you can easily achieve an authentic engraved look. Do try to choose a pale stone, however, which will help improve the text's legibility. I have used some Latin phrases in this project, but you could use phrases from any language.

Some stone is quite rough so you might need to apply a mist of turpentine to make sure the transfer has totally stuck into the surface; nevertheless, the technique is very easy.

Since this candleholder has four sides, you could choose expressions to suit your changing mood, so you might have a quotation or maxim that will cheer you up on one side, calm you down on another, and so on. Simply light a candle and turn the candleholder to the side you find most appropriate to your mood.

stone candleholder

You will need

Materials

Latin phrases (see page 93)

Access to a color photocopier

Lazertran transfer paper

Utility knife, metal ruler, and cutting mat,
   or a pair of scissors

2 shallow bowls

Paper towels

Pure turpentine

Small sponge roller

Cube-shaped stone candleholder

Soft cloth

Pump-action spray bottle

Technique

Wet-release transfer paper with turpentine
   (see page 10)

1 Choose an attractive typeface and type the words you want to appear on the candleholder. The Latin sentences used in this project are *imperium Oceano, famam qui terminet astris*, taken from the *Aeneid*, meaning "The Empire of Ocean, whose fame reached to the stars"; *si tu vales, ego gaudeo*, which translates as "If you are well, I am pleased"; and *ut seritur, ita metitur, which means* "As one sows, so does one reap".

This technique uses turpentine, so wear old clothes or an apron while you are working and make sure the room is well ventilated. Fit your chosen phrases on a sheet of paper and photocopy the sheet of phrases on the shiny side of some transfer paper. Print a couple more copies than you expect to use in case of mistakes. Using either a utility knife, metal ruler, and cutting mat, or a pair of scissors, trim around the text so each phrase will fit on one side of the candleholder.

2 Once you have decided on the position of your text, lower the first transfer into a shallow bowl of lukewarm water. The paper will start to roll up, but leave it to soak for a few minutes until it becomes less opaque. Lift the transfer out of the water and lay it face down on a layer of paper towels to remove excess water. Meanwhile, pour some pure turpentine into another bowl and use the sponge roller to apply the turpentine to one side of the candleholder.

3 Lift the transfer off the paper towels; then with your index fingers and thumbs, slide the backing paper off slightly. Lay the transfer face up (glue side down) on the surface you have turpentined and carefully slide out the backing paper. Once the text is in place, use a soft dry cloth to make sure the image is flat and secure with no air bubbles, then leave it to dry, lying flat. The transfer will start to melt and sink (migrate) into the surface.

Since the stone surface is quite rough, pour a little turpentine in a pump-action spray bottle and mist the transfer. Do not to spray the text too closely; too much turpentine will make the transfer break up. Repeat steps 2 and 3 with the remaining transfers. Once dry, the candleholder is ready for use.

Place mats are perfect for

transfers—they are flat, and therefore easy to work on, and they look lovely on a table set for a meal. You can purchase blanks—place mats that have already been cut and shaped—or you can make your own quite simply using thin plywood. The etching process used in this project is very simple, and a final coat of varnish will protect the mats for years to come.

floral place mats

The simple floral design used here, created from a pressed flower, provides a wonderful way to bring the outdoors into your home, or to give a constant memory of a special flower you grew or were given. Instead of repeating a single motif on all six mats, you could choose six related images that complement each other, such as six types of flower or six different leaves. You could also make a matching serving mat and some coasters to complete your set if you wish.

You will need

Materials

6 wooden place mats

Pale paint primer

2 tester jars of fast-drying water-based
   paint

Flat-ended 1 inch paintbrush

Pressed flower or picture of a pressed
   flower (see page 87)

Access to a color photocopier

Lazertran transfer paper

Utility knife and cutting mat, or a pair
   of scissors

2 shallow bowls

Pure turpentine

Small sponge roller

Paper towels

Clear spray varnish

Technique

Wet-release transfer paper with turpentine
   (see page 10)

1 This project involves the use of paint and turpentine, so wear old clothes or an apron while you are working and make sure the room is well ventilated. Paint each place mat with a coat of primer on one side and on all four edges. When the primer is dry, paint the place mats with two coats of fast-drying water-based paint in your chosen background color, leaving the mats to dry between each coat.

2 Fit six color copies of the flower on one sheet of paper—you could use a computer and scanner to aid this process, or you could color-photocopy the flower six times, cut them out, and glue them all on a blank sheet of paper.

Color-copy the sheet of images on the shiny side of a piece of transfer paper. Carefully cut out the flowers from the transfer paper using either a utility knife on a cutting mat, or scissors.

3 Pour a little pure turpentine into a small shallow bowl and, using a sponge roller, prepare the surface of the first place mat by applying a thin layer of turpentine to the area where the transfer will be positioned.

Place the first cutout image face down in a bowl of lukewarm water and leave it until the paper becomes less opaque. Lift the transfer out carefully; transfer paper tears easily, especially if the image is very delicate. Place it face down on a layer of paper towels to remove surface water. Ease off the backing paper between your index finger and thumb.

4 Depending on the intricacy of the image, use either your fingers or the tip of a scalpel to position the image face up (glue side down) on the mat. Gently remove any air bubbles with your fingertips and leave it to dry overnight. The transfer will melt and sink (migrate) into the surface of the mat. Repeat this process with the remaining place mats. Try to avoid overusing the turpentine, which can cause the image to disintegrate. Once the image has dried, coat the place mats with a layer of clear flat spray varnish to protect them.

Display your child's artwork

in a new and entertaining way. This project shows you how to decorate a plain office object in a way that will remind you of your children.

You could ask your child to draw a self-portrait or even a picture of what he or she thinks you look like. Alternatively, you could photocopy and transfer a special piece of artwork that your child has already completed.

Objects decorated with a child's drawing make great presents—your relatives will treasure them. Plain mouse pads are inexpensive and available from stationery and office suppliers.

The technique used in this project is simple to accomplish, but since a mouse pad needs to have an absolutely smooth surface, you will need to be especially careful to squeeze out all the air bubbles after you have removed the transfer's backing paper. If the mat begins to curl, wait until it dries and then place it under some heavy books for a few hours so the computer mouse will be able to glide easily over its surface when you use it.

mouse pad

You will need

Materials

Child's drawing

Access to a color photocopier

Lazertran transfer paper

Utility knife and cutting mat, or a pair
   of scissors

Large shallow tray

Pure turpentine

Small shallow bowl

Small sponge roller

Paper towels

Plastic mouse pad

Rolling pin

Technique

Wet release transfer paper with
   turpentine (see page 10)

3 Lift the transfer off the paper towels; then with your index fingers and thumbs, carefully slide the backing paper off slightly and lay the image face up (glue side down) on the mouse pad. Carefully slide out the backing paper and adjust the transfer's position. Use a rolling pin, in one direction only, to make sure the image is secure with no trapped air bubbles. Leave the mat to dry flat overnight. The transfer will sink (migrate) into the surface of the mouse pad which is then ready for use.

1 This technique involves the use of turpentine, so wear some old clothes or an apron when you are working and make sure the room is well ventilated. Color-copy the child's drawing, enlarging it or reducing it as necessary, so it fits fully on the surface of your mouse pad. Then, color-copy it on the shiny side of transfer paper. Trim your transfer to size, using either a utility knife on a cutting mat, or a pair of scissors.

2 Lower your image into a large shallow tray filled with lukewarm water. The paper will start to curl up slightly, but leave it to soak for a few minutes until it becomes less opaque. Pour some pure turpentine into a small shallow bowl and, using a sponge roller, apply a thin layer of turpentine to the surface of the mouse pad. Carefully lift the transfer out of the water and lay it face down on a layer of paper towels to remove any excess water.

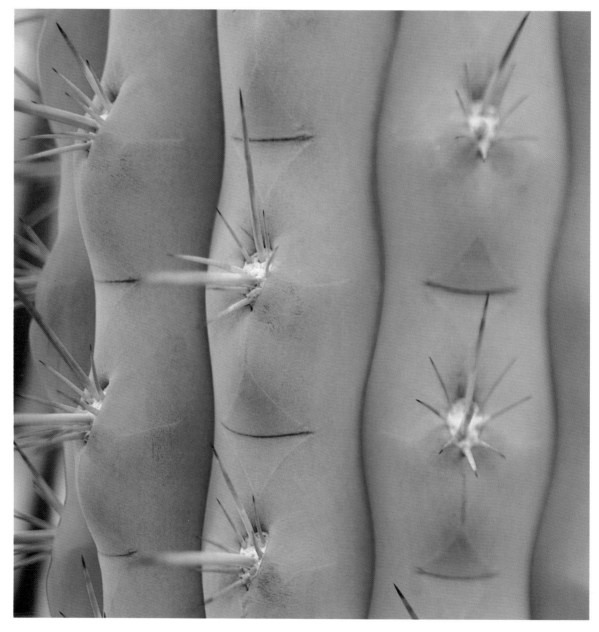

IMPERIUM OCEANO FAMAM QUI TERMINET ASTRIS

si tu vales, ego gaudeo

ut seritur, ita metitur

Page numbers in **bold** refer to the projects; illustrations are indicated in *italic*.

Published in North America in 2001 by
Laurel Glen Publishing
An imprint of the Advantage Publishers Group
5880 Oberlin Drive, San Diego, CA 92121
www.advantagebooksonline.com

First published in 2001 by Conran
Octopus Limited

Text and photography copyright
© 2001 Conran Octopus Ltd.
Project designs copyright
© 2001 Isabel de Cordova
Book design and layout copyright
© 2001 Conran Octopus Ltd.

All notations of errors or omissions should
be addressed to Laurel Glen Publishing,
editorial department, at the above
address. All other correspondence
(author inquiries, permissions and rights)
concerning the content of this book
should be addressed to: Conran
Octopus Ltd. ,2–4 Heron Quays,
London E14 4JP

ISBN 1-57145-582-5
Library of Congress Cataloging-in-
Publication Data available upon request
Printed in China

1 2 3 4 5   01 02 03 04 05

Publishing Director Lorraine Dickey
Commissioning Editor Emma Clegg
Senior Editor Katey Day
Editorial Assistant Ellie Hutt
Creative Director Leslie Harrington
Designer Nicky Collings
Photographer Sue Wilson
Stylists Isabel de Cordova and
Emily Jewsbury
Production Director Zoe Fawcett
Senior Production Controller
Manjit Sihra

Author's Acknowledgments

This book is dedicated to my mother,
Gillian de Cordova.

A big thank you to my family and
friends who all gave me invaluable
support in the creation of this book.
I would also like to acknowledge the
help of the team at Conran Octopus
for providing me with this opportunity
to publish my first book.

Suppliers

Most art shops will stock canvases,
turpentine, white craft glue, and spray
varnishes, and some will stock
Lazertran or ink-jet transfer paper
and Dylon transfer paste.
Alternatively, you could contact the
manufacturer for details of your
nearest retailer.

Lazertran Ltd
(wet-release transfer paper)
650 8th Avenue
New Hyde Park, NY 11040
Tel: 1-800-245-7547
Web site: www.lazertran.com
You can use Lazertran with the
following printers: Canon, Xerox,
Minolta, Ricoh (but not Hewlett
Packard).

Epson America, Inc.
(Iron on transfer paper)
3840 Kilroy Airport Way
Long Beach, CA 90806
Tel: (562) 981-3840
Web site: www.epson.com
You can use Epson Transfer paper with
the following printers: Epson Stylus
Color 400, 600, 800, and Epson Stylus
Photo.

Dylon—Color fun image maker—
(Fabric paste)
Dylon International Limited
Worsley Bridge Road
London SE26 5HD
Tel: 020 8663 4801
Website: www.dylon.co.uk

Photocopying—national
Kinko's
(Note—They will charge a computer
set-up fee if printing from a disk.)
Tel: 1-800-2-KINKOS
Website: www.kinkos.com

Arts & Crafts Supplies—national
Dick Blick Art Materials
Tel: 1-800-828-4548
Web site: www.dickblick.com

Jo-Ann Fabrics and Crafts
(Picture this Transfer)
Tel: 1-888-739-4120
Web site: www.joann.com

Michael's
Tel: 1-800-MICHAELS
Web site: www.michaels.com

Utrecht
Tel: 1-800-223-9132
Web site: www.utrechtart.com

Copyright-free images
Art Images for College Teaching
Tel. (612) 874-3781
Web site: www.mcad.edu/AICT

N.O.A.A. Photo Library
(among many other government
collections of free images)
Web site: www.photolib.noaa.gov

Public Domain Images
Tel: (202) 255-8063
Website: www.pdimages.com

Flame-Retardant Sprays
Flame Seal Products
Tel: (713) 668-4291
Web site: www.flameseal.com

National Fireproofing Company
Tel: 1-888-391-3981
Web site: www.natfire.com

FSI
Tel: 1-800-227 2694
Web site: www.fireprevention.com

Shops—national
(for inexpensive plain objects to use in
the projects)

Crate and Barrel
Tel: 1-800-967-6696
Web site: www.crateandbarrel.com

Ikea
Tel: 1-800-434-4532
Web site: www.ikea.com

Pottery Barn
Tel: 1-888-779-5176
www.potterybarn.com

Credits
Fork P1, P12, and P14—Dover
Publishing
Fob watch P15—Dover publishing
Picture of Children (Paula and Marc
Landau) P19, P26, P28, and P29—
Alistair Blair
Bed linen pattern P31, P32, and P33—
Dover publishing
Cactus, Bamboo, and Grass Reeds
P53—copyright © Octopus Publishing
Group/Peter Myers
Perfume image P58, P60, and P61—
copyright © Octopus Publishing
Group/Sandra Lane
Chef images P63, P64, P65—copyright
© Octopus Publishing Group/
Sandra Lane
Child's drawing P83, P84, and P85—
Heather Dunleavy